SCIENTIFIC
BREAKTHROUGHS

DISCOVERIES IN
PHYSICS
that changed the world

Rose Johnson

rosen publishing's
rosen
central

Published in 2015 by The Rosen Publishing Group, Inc.
29 East 21st Street, New York, NY 10010

© 2015 Brown Bear Books Ltd

First Edition

Library of Congress Cataloging-in-Publication Data
Johnson, Rose, 1981-
 Discoveries in physics that changed the world / Rose Johnson.
 -- First edition.
    pages cm. -- (Scientific breakthroughs)
Audience: Grades 5-8.
 Includes bibliographical references and index.
 ISBN 978-1-4777-8603-1 (library bound)
 1. Physics--Juvenile literature. 2. Discoveries in science--
Juvenile literature. I. Title.
 QC25.J64 2015
 530--dc23
                                    2014025364

Editor and Text: Rose Johnson
Editorial Director: Lindsey Lowe
Children's Publisher: Anne O'Daly
Design Manager: Keith Davis
Designers: Lynne Lennon and Jeni Child
Picture Researcher: Clare Newman
Picture Manager: Sophie Mortimer

Brown Bear Books has made every attempt to contact the copyright holder. If anyone has any information please contact:
licensing@brownbearbooks.co.uk

All artwork: © Brown Bear Books

Manufactured in Malaysia

Contents

Introduction

Physics explains how the universe works, from how balls bounce to why stars shine, using a set of unbreakable laws.

Physics is one of the oldest areas of science. As far back as the 6th century BCE, the philosophers of ancient Greece were trying to understand how the world worked simply by observing what it did. The word *physics* means "nature" in Greek. These philosophers had the idea that nature followed a set of rules that never changed. Since that time—and even today—scientists have been looking for these laws of physics.

Natural phenomena, such as lightning, can be explained in terms of physics.

Laws for everything

In the 17th century, Isaac Newton discovered the law of gravitation, which explains why objects fall to the ground and how the Moon orbits Earth. Other laws of physics cover how light, electricity, and magnets behave. Today's physicists are using a huge underground laboratory, called the Large Hadron Collider, to figure out some new rules. They want to know how matter (the material making up the universe) and energy (the property that makes matter move and change) are related—and where they came from in the first place.

Mother of science

Physics is not the only science, but its laws are used to create the foundation of all other sciences. For example, chemists study the properties of substances but they rely on physics to explain what everything is made up of. Without physics there could be no science at all.

5

The Archimedes Principle

This principle, attributed to the ancient Greek mathematician and inventor Archimedes, explains why some things float and others do not.

Legend has it that Archimedes was asked by the king to check whether a new crown was pure gold or if cheaper metals had been mixed into it. Gold has a higher density than cheaper metals, such as silver. (Density is a measure of how much matter is packed inside a substance.) A piece of gold weighs more than a piece of silver of the same size. Archimedes could not melt down the crown to measure its size and weight. But, then he had an idea in the bath.

FLOAT OR SINK?

When an object is immersed in a fluid it displaces, or pushes away, some of that fluid. The fluid also pushes back on the object with an equal force. If the weight of the object is greater than the displaced fluid, the object will sink. If it is lighter than the fluid, the object will float in or on top of the fluid.

A rubber duck is less dense than water, and weighs a lot less than the water it displaces—so it floats.

Archimedes is said to have shouted "Eureka!" (meaning "I have it!") after solving the problem as he stepped into his bath.

ARCHIMEDES

Archimedes was born in 287 BCE in Syracuse, a Greek city on the island of Sicily (now part of Italy). He figured out the Archimedes Principle in about 250 BCE. He is also famous for calculating the number π (pi) and inventing weapons that defeated a Roman invasion fleet in 214 BCE. He was murdered by a Roman soldier in 212 BCE.

Eureka moment!

As Archimedes got into the tub, he saw that his body displaced, or pushed out, some of the water. The volume of the displaced water must be the same as the volume of his body. Archimedes realized he could use this idea to measure the volume of the crown, and then calculate its density. When he did this he found that the crown had a lower density than pure gold. The king had been conned!

Extended version

Archimedes also realized that when an object is in water—or any fluid—the fluid is pushing against it. This force is named the buoyant force. The buoyant force is equal to the weight of the fluid displaced by the object. This simple link is known as the Archimedes Principle.

Law of Refraction

Beams of light can change direction as they shine through different materials. This phenomenon is called refraction.

The straw appears to shift as it goes underwater because the water is refracting, or redirecting, the light coming from it.

The study of light beams is called optics. Ancient scientists knew that light can change direction, by reflection and refraction. Reflection occurs when light hits a surface and bounces off in the opposite direction. During refraction, the light beam changes course slightly as it moves from one transparent medium, such as air, into another, such as water.

Optical effects

Different colors of light refract at different angles. Refraction creates rainbows and makes sunrises and sunsets appear red. A shimmering mirage is caused when light from the sky is refracted upward by a layer of warm air.

Refractive index

In 1621, Dutch mathematician Willebrord Snell (1580–1626) came up with a law for calculating how light beams refract. Every medium is given a number called a refractive index. The amount of refraction depends on the difference between the two numbers. The bigger the difference, the greater the change of angle as light passes from one medium to another. Although Snell did not know it, the refractive index is a measure of the speed of light through a medium. Light travels fastest in a vacuum, and slows down when it hits air, water, or glass. It is these changes in speed that create refraction.

IMPLICATIONS

Understanding refraction was crucial in making lenses. A lens works by refracting all the light that shines through it onto a single point. In other words, it focuses light. Focusing light can be used to intensify a beam or create a magnified view of a small or distant object.

A magnifying glass works by refracting an image so that it appears to be bigger.

Pressure and Vacuums

Pressure is a measure of how much force is pushing on a particular area. The ideas of gas pressure and vacuums are important for investigating physics.

A hurricane, like any storm, is produced by differences in air pressure that create winds—currents in the air.

The Greek philosopher Aristotle (384–322 BCE) said that a vacuum (a completely empty space) was not possible in nature. He said that as soon as the air (or another substance) was removed from a space, more would immediately rush in to replace it. However, by the 17th century, scientists in Europe began to question this theory.

Lifting water

Since ancient times, water was lifted over hills using a siphon. It was thought at the time that these tools worked by creating the beginnings of a vacuum. Water rushed in to fill it, and was sucked through the pipes in the process. However, there was a limit to how high siphons could pull water—about 33 feet (10 m).

Mercury tubes

In 1643, Italian scientist Evangelista Torricelli (1608–1647) tried to find out the reason for this limit. Instead of water, he used mercury, a liquid metal that is 14 times denser than water. He poured mercury into a long glass tube, which was sealed at one end. He put the open end in a bath of mercury

Weather maps have isobars, or pressure contours. Wherever the isobars are close together, the winds will be strong.

IMPLICATIONS

Torricelli's mercury tube was the first barometer—a device for measuring air pressure. Today, barometers are used to forecast the weather. A weather map is covered in lines called isobars, which show how the air pressure changes from place to place. Low pressure means rain, while high pressure creates sunny weather.

Evangelista Torricelli found that something was pushing the mercury up inside a glass tube.

and measured how high up the
tube the liquid went. He found it
was about 30 inches (76 cm)—a
14th as high as the water in a
siphon. The level of mercury rose
and fell slightly from day to day.
This showed that whatever force
was causing the liquid to move could change.

The air pressure at
the top of Mount
Everest is one third
of the pressure at
sea level.

Air pressure

After Torricelli died, Blaise Pascal took over the
research. Pascal thought it was not a vacuum pulling
the mercury up the tube but the weight of the air
pushing down on the mercury bath and forcing the
liquid to rise up the tube. In 1648 Pascal arranged
for a mercury tube to be carried up a mountain in
central France. The height of the mercury dropped
as it was taken higher. Pascal was right. At higher
altitudes, there was less air to push down on
the mercury, so it rose to a lower height. Pascal's

discovery also explained the siphon limit. It was air pressure that was pushing water through siphons—and it was never strong enough to push it higher than around 33 feet (10 m). Today pressure is measured in units called Pascals (Pa).

Empty space

So what was in the space above the mercury inside the tube? Could it be nothing at all—a vacuum? In 1650, German inventor Otto von Guericke (1602–1686) showed that vacuums were indeed possible. He used a pump to remove all the air from inside two metal hemispheres that fitted together. The pressure pushing out from the inside was zero, and so the air pressure pushing on the outside locked the hemispheres together very tightly. Even teams of horses could not pull them apart!

FACTS

- The pressure 330 feet (100 m) underwater is 10 times higher than at the surface.
- Sound is a wave in air and so it cannot travel through a vacuum. However, light can shine through it.
- Blaise Pascal also invented the roulette wheel.

Air pressure pushed Von Guericke's hemispheres together so tightly that two teams of eight horses could not pull them apart.

Pendulums

The back-and-forth swinging of a pendulum is an example of oscillation. Oscillations are seen in many areas of physics, including the way atoms vibrate.

There is a story that the great Italian scientist Galileo Galilei (1564–1642). was watching a lamp swing in Pisa Cathedral, Italy. The lamp was set swinging by a priest as he lit its candles. The swing was wide at first but gradually became smaller. However, Galileo noticed that the time it took for the lamp to complete each swing (known as its period) always stayed the same. Twenty years later, in 1602, Galileo did more research and found that the period was proportional to the square root of the length of the pendulum. The weight on the end had no effect.

A pendulum always swings at a set rate, and so can be used to control a clock.

Keeping time

That fact meant that all pendulums of the same length swung with the same rhythm. In 1656, Dutch scientist Christiaan Huygens (1629–1695) used this fact to design a pendulum clock. The pendulum's period was set to one second—the bob, or weight, on the end of the pendulum could be raised or lowered to fine tune it. Each swing controlled "clockwork" cogs that moved the minute hand after 60 swings.

Oscillators

Later clock designs used springs. A weight bouncing up and down on a spring is oscillating in the same way as a pendulum. This kind of motion is also used to understand the way atoms vibrate when they are bonded to each other, and how some type of electric currents flow.

HARMONIC MOTION

The swing of a pendulum is simple harmonic motion (SHM). Musical sound waves, or harmonics, vibrate in the same way, and that is where the name for the motion comes from. SHM is produced by a force that is always pulling a mass back to a central point. The force gets bigger as the mass moves farther from the central point, causing the mass to swing one way and then the next.

A pogo stick is an example of an oscillating spring. It will keep bouncing until you stop or fall off.

The Gas Laws

All gases share a number of properties. The three gas laws describe the links between the temperature, pressure, and volume of a gas.

There are three main states of matter: solid, liquid, and gas. Solids and liquids have fixed volumes. However, gases do not, and so spread out to fill the entire volume of whatever container they are in.

Boyle's Law

In the 1660s, the Irish-born scientist Robert Boyle (1627–1691) discovered that the volume of a gas was inversely proportional to its pressure. In other words, the pressure of a fixed amount of gas goes up as it is made to fill a smaller space. This relationship is known as Boyle's Law. It tells us that a gas is made up of invisible particles, and these exert pressure

A gas is stored at high pressure inside a spray can. As the gas is released, the gas pressure drops, and its volume goes up—creating the spray.

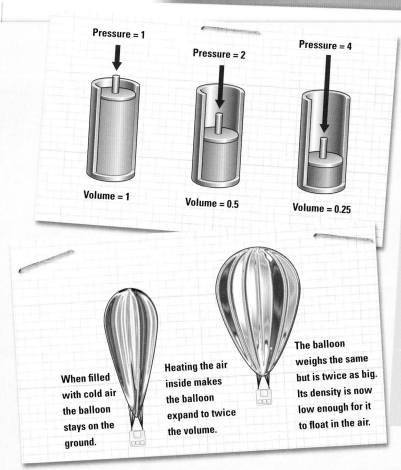

Pressure = 1
Volume = 1

Pressure = 2
Volume = 0.5

Pressure = 4
Volume = 0.25

Boyle's Law: Squeezing a gas makes the volume go down.

When filled with cold air the balloon stays on the ground.

Heating the air inside makes the balloon expand to twice the volume.

The balloon weighs the same but is twice as big. Its density is now low enough for it to float in the air.

Charles' Law: Heating a gas makes it expand.

THREE LAWS

Boyle's Law (1660) states that $P \propto 1/V$. Gas pressure (P) is inversely proportional to its volume (V).
Charles's Law (1780) states that $V \propto T$. The volume of a gas (V) is proportional to its temperature (T).
Gay-Lussac's Law (1802) states that $P \propto T$. Gas pressure (P) is proportional to temperature (T). (The symbol $\propto$ means "is proportional to.")

by colliding with a surface. If the particles are squeezed into a smaller space, they collide with the container more often, and the pressure goes up.

Two more laws

About 100 years later, two more gas laws were revealed. Charles's Law says that the volume of a gas increases with temperature (if the pressure stays the same). This law tells us that a gas's particles move and spread out faster when it is hot. Gay-Lussac's Law says that gas pressure increases with temperature (and the volume stays the same). This is because the particles move around more quickly and collide with the container more often—creating greater pressure.

Universal Gravity

Gravity is the force that makes things fall to the ground. It also keeps the Moon orbiting Earth.

We now know that gravity is the force that holds together the universe, but before some brilliant discoveries in the 17th century, this fact was not understood. In the 1600s, Italian scientist Galileo Galilei discovered the "Law of Fall," which states that the distance an object falls is proportional to the square of the time it falls. That shows that the speed at which an object falls keeps on increasing. In other words, it accelerates toward the ground.

Newton's apple

The famous story about the discovery of how gravity works

Gravity is the force between all objects in the Universe. It holds the Moon in orbit around Earth.

Sir Isaac Newton was the first scientist to come up with a complete theory of gravity.

ISAAC NEWTON

English scientist Isaac Newton studied at Cambridge University, England. His book *Mathematical Principles of Natural Philosophy* was published in 1687. It explains how the force that makes objects fall to the ground also controls the motion of Earth and the other planets. Newton also investigated the nature of light *and* invented calculus, a form of math that allows us to explain complex natural systems using numbers.

tells how the English physicist Isaac Newton (1642–1727) was sitting under a tree in 1665 when an apple fell from a branch to the ground. In that instant, Newton is said to have realized how the force of gravity was acting on the apple, and on a larger scale, how that same force was at work in keeping the planets in orbit around the Sun.

Gravitational forces

Newton's theory of gravity, or gravitation, was that gravity is a force of attraction that pulls all matter together. There is a gravitational force between any two objects in the universe, no matter how large or small. Newton showed that objects attract each other with a force that depends on the masses of the objects and the distance between them.

A surfer straddles his center of gravity. If he is too far forward or back the board will tip.

Heavier masses make a bigger force. The greater the distance between the objects, the smaller the force of gravity pulling them together. Gravity is actually the weakest force in the universe. However, there is so much matter in planets and stars that their gravity is powerful enough to act over huge distances. So the gravity of Earth pulls smaller masses (such as our bodies) to its surface, while the gravity of the Sun holds Earth in orbit around it.

Mass and weight

People often use the word *weight* to describe how heavy an object is. Scientists prefer to talk about *mass*. Mass is the amount of matter something contains. In science *weight* is a measure of the force of gravity pulling on a mass. An object's mass is the same no matter where it is in the universe, but the weight changes. Earth is more massive than the Moon, so its gravity is more powerful. The Moon exerts less of a pull on objects. A person on the Moon has the same mass but weighs about a sixth of what he or she weighs on Earth.

Center of gravity

Every object has a center of gravity. This point is where all the forces of gravity acting on the object are concentrated. A balanced object has its center of gravity directly above where it touches the ground. However, if the center of gravity is to one side, the pull of gravity will make the object topple over. The most stable objects have a low center of gravity.

IMPLICATIONS

Universal gravitation works very well for most objects. It explains the path of a bullet fired from a gun, Earth's tides, and how astronauts can walk in space. But it doesn't work for massive objects or for objects that are traveling near the speed of light. Another theory was needed here—Albert Einstein's theory of relativity.

Although he appears to be floating in space, gravity from the Earth is acting on this astronaut; it stops him from flying out into space.

The Laws of Motion

Objects move and change direction when forces act on them. There are three simple rules that govern how all objects—from pool balls to rockets—behave.

Motion is when a mass changes its position in space over time. The rate at which it changes its position is called the speed. When speed is measured in a certain direction it is known as velocity. That means a car turning a corner will change its velocity but not necessarily its speed—its direction changes, not how fast it is going.

Applying force

A change in velocity is called an acceleration. This word often refers to an object moving faster, but in physics it can also mean the object is slowing or changing direction. For an object to

A game of pool is all about applying the right amount of force in the right direction to move a ball into a pocket.

The third law explains how a rocket takes off. The rocket pushes the hot gas backward and the hot gas pushes the rocket forward.

THE THREE LAWS

First Law: An object at rest will stay at rest, and an object in motion will stay in motion, unless a force acts on it.

Second Law (F=ma): The acceleration (a) of an object is proportional to the magnitude of a force (F) and inversely proportional to the mass (m) of the object.

Third Law: Every action (force) has an equal and opposite reaction (force).

accelerate, a force must be applied to it. Forces can be produced in a number of ways, but they all obey the three Laws of Motion.

Newton's laws

The Laws of Motion were described by the English scientist Isaac Newton in 1687. The first law says that a mass has inertia, which means that it stays in its state of motion—either moving or staying still—until a force acts on it to change that state. The second law uses the formula F=ma (force=mass times acceleration) to relate how force accelerates a mass. A large force will create a larger acceleration than a smaller one; while a large mass needs a bigger force to accelerate it than a small one. The final law says that a force acting on an object always results in an equal force pushing back the other way.

Latent Heat

Adding heat to a substance does not always make its temperature go up. This hidden heat tells us about the way matter is structured.

Matter changes state as it gets hotter or colder. The coldest state is solid. As it gets warmer a solid melts into a liquid, which in turn boils into a gas. Every substance has its own particular melting and boiling temperature. Accurate thermometers (for measuring temperature) were invented in the 1750s, and scientists began to use them to record the precise melting and boiling points of different materials.

Latent heat explains why snow takes a long time to thaw, even after the weather warms up. The ice stays as a solid until it receives enough energy to break up into liquid water.

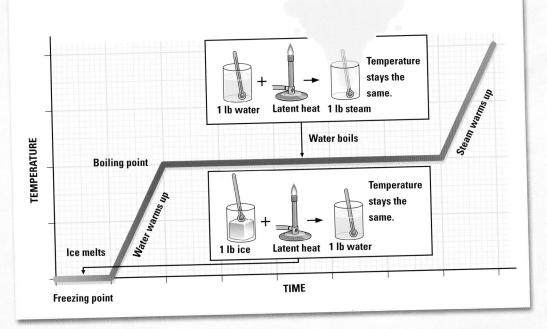

Hidden energy

A Scottish doctor named Joseph Black (1728–1799) found that as ice was melting, its temperature did not go up until it had all become water—even though heat was being added by a flame. The same thing happened when water boiled into steam. Black termed this effect "latent heat."

Breaking bonds

When a solid is heated, the particles inside it move around faster. Eventually the bonds connecting the particles begin to break, and it becomes a liquid. Adding more heat makes all the bonds break, and the liquid becomes gas. Latent heat is the energy needed to break the bonds that hold the material together.

This graph shows how the temperature changes as you heat a pound of ice. When the temperature stays the same, latent heat is being added.

FACTS

- Joseph Black began studying heat after seeing how snow did not melt very quickly after the weather warmed up.
- The word *latent* means to "lie hidden." Every substance has specific values for latent heat.

25

Electric Current

Electricity is a build up of charge. If a supply of charge can be made to flow through a substance, it forms a current.

The field of physics that looks at electricity is called electromagnetism. It is based on a simple rule: Opposites attract and like charges repel. This rule applies to magnets—a north pole attracts a south pole but repels a north—as well as to electricity. The ancient Greeks had studied static electricity, where objects could be made to attract and repel each other. They did not understand it in terms of charge. That idea was proposed by American Benjamin Franklin (1706–1790) in the 1750s.

LUIGI GALVANI

Born in Bologna, Italy, in 1737, Luigi Galvani qualified as a medical doctor. He specialized as a surgeon and became an expert in anatomy working at the University of Bologna. He discovered "animal electricity" while preparing frog specimens for dissection. He died in 1798.

Luigi Galvani discovered electric current by experimenting with the legs of frogs.

Giving the body a static charge makes the hairs repel each other—creating an amazing hairstyle!

Animal electricity

In 1780, Italian scientist Luigi Galvani discovered a way of making electric charge flow as a current. Having studied the anatomy of frogs, he believed that animal tissue itself might contain electricity. To prove this theory, he made a curved rod with copper at one end and iron at the other. Touching this rod to a pair of frog's legs made the legs twitch. Galvani had not only found that muscles worked using electricity, he had also made a simple electric battery. The current was created by the two metals reacting and releasing charged particles that flowed through the frog's legs.

Voltaic pile

Another Italian, Alessandro Volta (1745–1827), copied the system to build the first real battery. Piles of metal discs (silver and zinc) were separated by paper soaked in salt water (instead of the frog). When the top of the pile was connected to the bottom with a wire, the metals began to react with each other, and sent a current of electric charge through the pile.

CONDUCTORS AND INSULATORS

In 1730, English scientist Stephen Gray had shown that some materials (insulators) blocked electricity while others (conductors) let it flow. A modern electric cable (below) has copper conductors surrounded by plastic insulators.

27

Nature of Light

What is light made of? Some scientists said it was a stream of particles that bounced around like balls; others said it was a wave, rippling though space.

In the 17th century, two of Europe's greatest scientists put forward different theories about the nature of light. Following his experiments in 1665 and 1666, Isaac Newton proposed that light was made of tiny particles, which bounced around according to the same laws that controlled motion in larger objects.

Another view

Dutchman Christiaan Huygens (1629–1695) said that light was a wave. Light waves traveled out in all direction from a light source, such as a star or candle flame, like the ripples on a pond.

Isaac Newton studied light by blacking out his living room and letting in a single beam of light.

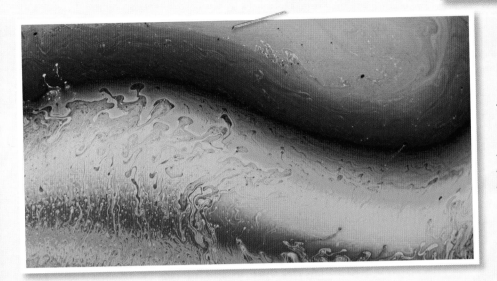

This colorful pattern is created by the interference of light that is reflecting off a thin layer of gasoline floating on top of water.

Double slit

In 1801, a simple experiment proved one of these theories. The experiment was performed by Englishman Thomas Young (1773–1829). He shined a light through two narrow slits in a board. That split the light into two beams, which shone through the slits on to a screen. Young saw that the beams created a pattern of light and dark bands on the screen. This pattern was created by interference, which is a property of waves.

Interference

As a wave moves forward, it oscillates from a high point (or crest) to a low point and back again. When two waves meet they merge together. If the wave crests meet, they combine to make a bigger wave, seen as a brighter light. If a crest meets a dip, the waves cancel each other out. The light beams from the slits were doing both these things and thus created the light and dark bands. Light, therefore, must be a wave.

FACTS

- A wavelength is the distance between the crests of a wave.
- Our eyes show light of different wavelengths as different colors.
- Red light has the longest wavelength. Blue light has the shortest wavelength. Green light is in the middle.

29

Electromagnetic Induction

Electricity and magnets are two aspects of the same property of matter. Their relationship can be harnessed to power machines.

I n 1820, Danish college professor Hans Christian Ørsted (1777–1851) was giving his students a lecture about how an electric current could make a wire heat up. As he demonstrated this, a compass on the desk swung around to point at the electrified wire. By accident, Ørsted had discovered that electrified objects became magnetic. However, when the current was turned off, the magnetic effects ended.

Michael Faraday began a tradition of giving Christmas science lectures at London's Royal Institution.

MICHAEL FARADAY

Michael Faraday was born in London, England, in 1791. In 1813 he became the assistant to Humphry Davy, the most famous scientist in the world at the time. Based on an idea by Davy, Faraday invented the first working electric motor in 1823. Eight years later he discovered electromagnetic induction and built the first electricity generator.

Electromagnetism

Ørsted's discovery began a field of physics called electromagnetism, which looks at how electricity and magnetism are connected. One of the first advances was the electromagnet. This device was invented in 1824 and contained a piece of iron with a copper wire wrapped around it. When the wire was electrified, the iron became a powerful magnet.

Bumper cars are powered by electric motors. The motor converts an electric current runnnig down the pole from an electrified grid on the ceiling into motion.

The motor effect

In 1823, English scientist Michael Faraday investigated how electric currents and magnetic fields could be used to make motion. A magnet has two poles, where the force field is more powerful. One of the poles is termed north, the other, south. Opposite poles attract each other, while like poles repel. Faraday managed to control the magnetic forces acting between an electromagnet and a regular magnet to create a simple motor that spun around.

Wind turbines convert the motion of the wind into electricity. The fans spin magnets inside, inducing an electrical current in a conductor.

Inducing currents

In 1831, Faraday made another discovery. When a metal wire (or other conductor) is placed in a moving magnetic field, a current begins to flow through it. Faraday named this phenomenon electromagnetic induction. Electrical generators in power plants use induction to produce the electrical power that drives our machines. Michael Faraday had invented the first generator.

Changing fields

The motor effect and induction are both the result of the interaction of electrical and magnetic force fields—the areas around objects where forces are working. The motor effect converts the energy in an electrical current into a force that creates motion. Induction converts the energy of motion into

Transformers are used to control voltage, the force that pushes along an electric current.

a force that pushes an electrical current through a conductor. The important feature is that these fields are frequently changing their position in relation to each other, and it is these changes that keep producing the forces.

Joseph Henry

American physicist Joseph Henry (1797–1878) discovered induction at the same time as Faraday. He invented electromagnetic switches used in telegraph machines and early telephones and computers.

James Clerk Maxwell

In 1864, Scottish physicist James Clerk Maxwell (1831–1879) figured out the math behind electromagnetism. That showed him that light was linked to electromagnetism. A beam of light is a vibrating electromagnetic force field traveling through space.

TRANSFORMERS

The force that pushes electric currents down wires is measured as voltage. Power cables use a high voltage to transmit currents, but electrical devices need a small voltage. Devices called transformers use induction to alter the voltage. A transformer has an iron ring with two wire coils wrapped around it. A current arriving in the first coil induces a current in the second one, which flows out the other side. If the first coil has more turns than the second one, the voltage of the current is reduced as it is transferred to the second coil. If the second coil has the most turns in it, the voltage will be increased by the transformer.

The Conservation of Energy

Energy cannot be created or destroyed. The amount always stays the same. However, it can be changed from one form to another.

In physics, the term "work" means to use a force to move or rearrange matter. To do work, you need a supply of energy. Energy can take many forms, which can change from one form into another. For example, an electricity generator converts motion energy (also called kinetic energy) into electrical energy. An electric motor does the opposite, converting electrical energy into motion.

Drag racers have huge engines that convert the heat from burning fuel into motion.

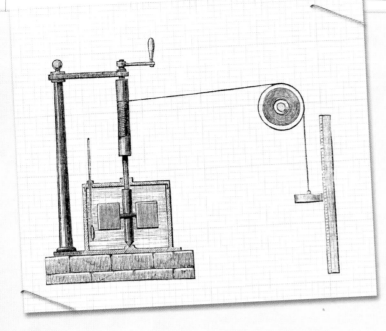

James Joules's apparatus measured how motion could be converted into heat.

Useful energy

An engine converts the energy from burning fuel into motion. However, that motion always stops unless more fuel energy is added. Engines do not run forever once they are started up. This fact is not because the energy is disappearing, but because it is escaping as heat—instead of being used to make motion. In the 1840s, the English scientist James Joules (1818–1889) showed that energy is conserved, meaning the total amount of all kinds of energy stays the same.

Measuring energy

In 1843, Joules built an apparatus where a pulley system attached a weight to a stirrer in a tank of water. When the weight dropped, it made the stirrer spin at high speed. Joules showed that this stirring motion heated up the water, and that the same amount of motion energy always produced the same rise in temperature. The unit of energy is named the joule (J) in his honor.

IMPLICATIONS

The work of James Joules and others showed that mechanical devices could not make use of all the energy they were given. Some energy was always lost by making the machine heat up. Early steam locomotives used about 10 percent of their energy to create motion. Modern machines are a bit more efficient. A gasoline engine is about 25 percent efficient, while a hybrid car's engines will use around 45 percent of its energy supply.

The Electron

For a long time it was thought that it was impossible to have matter any smaller than an atom. The electron was the first subatomic particle to be discovered.

The English physicist J.J. Thomson used this vacuum tube (below) to show that electrons were particles smaller than atoms.

In 1869, English physicist William Crookes (1832–1919) investigated how electricity works in a vacuum. He sucked the air out of a sealed glass tube and added positive and negative electrodes (known as the anode and cathode respectively). When he ran electricity between the electrodes, Crookes found his tube produced an invisible beam that flowed from the cathode to the anode, and then carried on to the end of the tube. Crookes showed that this "cathode ray" could produce a glow. It would also bend in a magnetic field and could even make a little paddlewheel fitted inside the tube spin around.

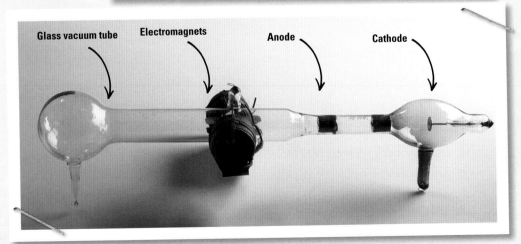

Glass vacuum tube   Electromagnets   Anode   Cathode

The first TV sets made a picture by scanning a flickering beam of electrons on to the back of the screen. The beam made up a picture out of a pattern of glowing dots.

FACTS

- An electric current is a stream of electrons flowing through a wire.
- There is a very rare form of electron that has a positive charge. It is called a positron.
- Electrons are found in all atoms. Every element's atoms have a particular number. Hydrogen atoms have one electron, while uranium atoms have 92.
- The word electron comes from the Greek for "amber." This unusual stone was used in ancient times to investigate electrical effects.

Stream of particles

The evidence suggested that cathode rays were made up of particles. They couldn't be radio waves because other invisible forms of light are not affected by magnetic fields. They also do not push against solid surfaces (as in the paddlewheel experiment).

Smaller than an atom

In 1899, English scientist J.J. Thomson (1856–1940) used Crookes's tube to test if cathode rays were affected by electric fields. The ray moved, swinging toward the positive side of the electric field. That meant it was negatively charged (opposite charges attract each other). Thomson then compared how much a magnetic field deflected the ray with the deflection from the electric field. That allowed him to work out the weight of the particles, which he named electrons. One electron was nearly 2,000 times lighter than the smallest atom!

Speed of Light

The speed of light is the top speed of the universe. Albert Einstein revealed that traveling close to the speed of light has some very weird effects.

In 1905, German-born American scientist Albert Einstein (1879–1955) changed physics all by himself when he published his theory of relativity. The theory's main statement was that the speed of light was constant and that nothing could travel faster than that speed.

On a beam of light

Einstein began thinking about this idea as a teenager, when he asked himself what he would see if he could sit on a beam of light. The obvious answer would be that he could see light arriving from the front, but if he turned around, it would be black. Light coming

Albert Einstein's theory of relativity changed our understanding of how the Universe works on the largest scales.

from behind would be traveling at the same speed as his beam and so it would not be able to catch up—and so his eyes would not see it.

The theory of relativity

However, Einstein explained that no matter how fast a light source was traveling compared to an observer—either toward him or her or away—the light always arrived at exactly the same speed. For light speed to be fixed, space and time have to change shape, or warp, instead. As an object travels faster, the space it occupies shrinks. It also moves through time more slowly, and even gets heavier. Relativity also used space warps to explain gravity. Massive objects had stronger gravity because they curved the space around them more than lighter ones did.

The red car lights are moving away, while the white ones are moving toward us—but the light from both arrives at the same speed.

IMPLICATIONS

The effects of relativity are too tiny for us to notice in our everyday lives. However, we can measure them when we look at very large and very fast objects. For example, clocks slow down when they are put inside high-speed aircraft. They are working perfectly, it is just that time is slower on the aircraft than it is on the ground.

Atomic Structure

Ernest Rutherford (right) and Hans Geiger pose with the equipment they used to discover the atomic nucleus.

Atoms are the units that make up the substances around us. There are about 90 types, but they are all built using the same subatomic particles.

The Universe contains about 90 substances called elements (a few more are made in laboratories). An element is a special material that cannot be divided into simpler constituents. Elements can, however, combine with each other to make more complex substances called compounds. For example, water is a compound of the elements hydrogen and oxygen, while sodium and chlorine combine to make salt. The atoms of an element have a specific structure, which gives each substance a unique set of properties—making gold a heavy metal or sulfur a yellow powder. However, all atoms are formed from the same basic particles.

Charged particles

The first subatomic particle to be discovered was the electron. The electron is negatively charged, and when one is removed from an atom, the matter left behind becomes positively charged. J.J. Thomson, who discovered the electron, thought the atom was like a "plum pudding" with the negatively charged electrons dotted around like plums in a positively charged "dough."

Atomic nucleus

In 1909, the New Zealand physicist Ernest Rutherford (1871–1937) thought the plum pudding idea must be wrong because atoms could give out positively charged particles (known as alpha particles) as well as negatively

FACTS

- The first scientist to show that substances are made up of different atoms bonded together was Englishman John Dalton in 1803.
- The word atom comes from ancient Greek. It means "uncuttable."
- The atoms of each element have a specific mass. The smallest and lightest atom is the hydrogen atom. One of the heaviest ones is uranium.

The ideas of how atoms are structured have changed a lot over the last 200 years.

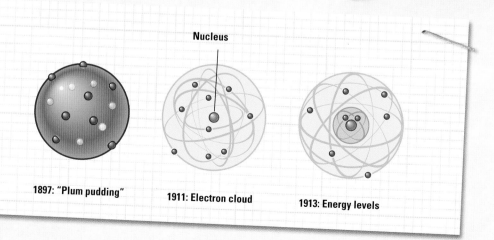

Nucleus

1897: "Plum pudding"

1911: Electron cloud

1913: Energy levels

41

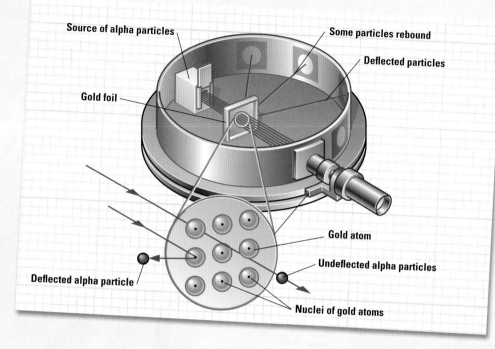

Source of alpha particles

Some particles rebound

Deflected particles

Gold foil

Gold atom

Undeflected alpha particles

Deflected alpha particle

Nuclei of gold atoms

In Rutherford's experiment, a beam of alpha particles was fired at a piece of gold foil. The results led to a new model of atomic structure.

charged ones. Rutherford was helped to carry out an experiment by German physicist Hans Geiger (1882–1945). They fired alpha particles at a thin piece of gold foil. Most of the alpha particles went straight through the foil. A few alpha particles bounced back. That told Rutherford that most of the atom was empty space. The results led Rutherford to propose a new atomic model in 1911. The revised version had a positively charged nucleus clustered in the middle, with electrons moving in orbits around the outer edge of the atom.

IMPLICATIONS

The way subatomic particles behave is very different to the large-scale world in which we live. Quantum physics explains that particles are not blobs of matter. They are a pattern of different characteristics, such as charge, speed, and spin, which can exist in several forms at once. It is impossible to know where the particle is or what it is doing all at the same time.

Nuclear particles

Rutherford showed that the positive nucleus was made up of particles called protons, and the atom also had extra mass in the form of neutrons, which were neutral (non-charged) particles. The three subatomic particles helped to explain radioactivity, which had been discovered in 1896 by Frenchman Henri Becquerel (1852–1908). Radioactivity occurs in unstable atoms, where the nucleus fires out different clusters of charged particles.

Bohr's atomic model

In 1913, Danish physicist Niels Bohr updated our view of the atom—and we still use his version today. He found that electrons jumped around inside the atom as they absorbed and released energy in the form of light or other radiation. Each electron can absorb certain wavelengths of light and that makes it move farther out from the nucleus. When it drops back to its original position, the electron releases the light again. This idea was an early example of quantum physics.

NIELS BOHR

Bohr was born in Copenhagen, Denmark, in 1885. He proposed his atomic model in 1913 and soon after he was asked to set up the physics institute in Copenhagen—still a leading center in quantum physics. In 1943 he helped 7,000 Danish Jews escape from the Nazis, and then he fled to the United States. He died back in Copenhagen in 1960.

Niels Bohr was a founding figure in the field of quantum physics.

Nuclear Fission

Some of the largest explosions ever were caused by nuclear fission. This process makes atomic nuclei split apart and release a huge amount of energy.

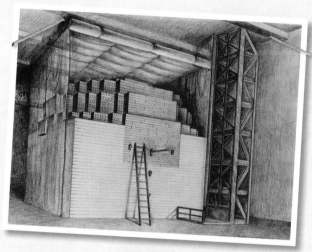

The first nuclear reactor was called Pile-1. It was built in a racquet ball court at the University of Chicago.

Nuclear fission is a kind of radioactivity. Most radioactivity that occurs naturally involves small particles being flung out of an unstable nucleus. Nuclear fission involves a large atom splitting into two smaller atoms. Fission is rare in nature, but in the 1930s, physicists discovered how it do it artificially.

NUCLEAR FUSION

In the 1940s another type of nuclear reaction was discovered. Nuclear fusion involves two small atoms being smashed together so hard that they merge, or fuse, to make one larger atom. Fusion is even more powerful than fission. Fusion deep inside the Sun produces all its light and heat.

Splitting atoms

Italian-born American physicist Enrico Fermi (1901–1954) had the idea of firing neutrons at atoms to see what would happen. Other scientists copied his experiment and found that new elements appeared inside samples of uranium after they had been bombarded. They realized that a neutron had entered a type of uranium atom (U-235). That had made it so unstable it had split into smaller atoms by nuclear fission.

Chain reaction

The fission of U-235 releases neutrons, which go on to cause more atoms to split in a chain reaction. In 1942, Fermi built the first nuclear reactor in Chicago. It used blocks of carbon to absorb some of the neutrons and slow down the fission reaction so it did not explode. Nuclear reactors are used today to release heat from fission. The heat is used to generate electricity. A fast chain reaction is used in atomic bombs to create an enormous explosion.

FACTS

- The Manhattan Project was the code name for the U.S. operation to build the first nuclear bombs powered by fission.
- An eighth of the world's electricity supply is produced using nuclear power plants.

An uncontrolled fission reaction produces a huge explosion that creates a mushroom-shaped cloud.

TIMELINE

c. 250 BCE: Archimedes discovers the buoyancy principle, which explains why things float.

1602 CE: Galileo figures out the relationship between the length of a pendulum and how long it takes to make a swing.

1621: Willebrord Snell proposes the Law of Refraction.

1643: Evangelista Torricelli invents the first barometer for measuring air pressure.

1648: Blaise Pascal proves that air pressure drops with altitude.

1656: Christiaan Huygens designs the first pendulum clocks.

1660: Robert Boyle discovers the first gas law: the volume of a gas is inversely proportional to its pressure.

1665: Isaac Newton formulates the Universal Law of Gravitation.

1687: Newton presents his three Laws of Motion.

1750s: Joseph Black discovers latent heat involved in changing states of matter.

1780: Luigi Galvani discovers an electric current.

1801: Thomas Young shows that light is a wave.

1820: Hans Christian Ørsted discovers that electrified objects have a magnetic field.

1831: Michael Faraday discovers electromagnetic induction.

1843: James Joules shows that motion energy can be converted into heat.

1899: J.J. Thomson find the electron, the first subatomic particle.

1905: Albert Einstein presents the theory of relativity.

1909: The atomic nucleus is discovered.

1942: The first controlled nuclear fission reaction takes place.

1945: First atomic bomb used.

GLOSSARY

acceleration: When an object changes its velocity.

altitude: A measure of height above sea level.

buoyant force: The force that pushes on a solid object immersed in a fluid, such as water.

charge: A property of electricity that makes things positively or negatively charged.

conductor: A substance that carries an electric current.

density: A measure of how much matter is packed into a volume.

energy: A property needed to alter the motion or state of matter.

inertia: The way matter resists changes to its motion.

insulator: A substance that blocks the flow of electric currents.

interference: When waves merge together.

mass: A measure of how much matter is in an object.

medium: A background material that carries waves.

nucleus: An atom's central core.

oscillator: An object that vibrates.

radioactivity: When an unstable atom breaks apart.

subatomic: Smaller than an atom.

vacuum: A space with nothing in it.

weight: A measure of the force of gravity pulling on a mass.

FOR MORE INFORMATION

BOOKS

Cooper, Christopher. *The Basics of Nuclear Physics*. New York: Rosen Publishing, 2015.

Holl, Kristi. *Discovering the Nature of Gravity*. New York: Rosen Publishing, 2015.

Pohlen, Jerome. *Albert Einstein and Relativity for Kids: His Life and Ideas with 21 Activities and Thought Experiments*. Chicago: Chicago Review Press, 2012.

WEB SITES

Because of the changing nature of Internet links, Rosen Publishing has developed an online list of websites related to the subject of this book. This site is updated regularly. Please use this link to access this list:

http://www.rosenlinks.com/SCIB/Phys

INDEX